# COCK
## -A-
# DOODLE

COCK-A-DOODLE

An Hachette UK Company
www.hachette.co.uk

Summersdale Publishers Ltd
Part of Octopus Publishing Group Limited
Carmelite House
50 Victoria Embankment
LONDON
EC4Y 0DZ
UK

www.summersdale.com

Printed and bound in China

ISBN: 978-1-80007-981-6

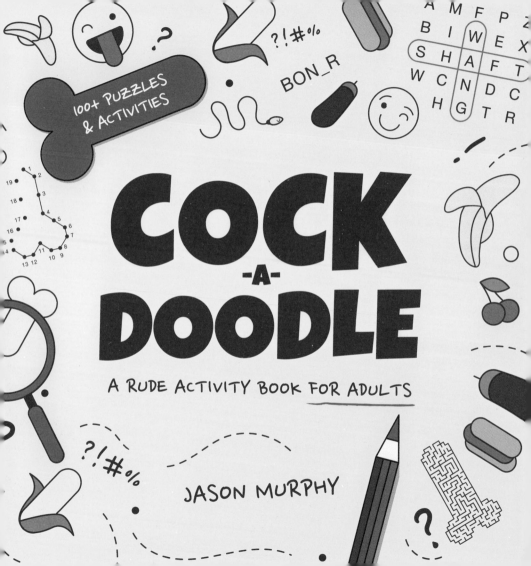

100+ PUZZLES & ACTIVITIES

BON_R

| A | M | F | P | Z |
|---|---|---|---|---|
| B | I | W | E | X |
| S | H | A | F | T |
| W | C | N | D | C |
| H | G | T | R |   |

# COCK
## -A-
# DOODLE

A RUDE ACTIVITY BOOK FOR ADULTS

JASON MURPHY

TO: _____

From: _____

I bought you this book because I know you love

_____ and _____

WELCOME TO

# COCK-A-DOODLE

### THE ACTIVITY BOOK WITH A DEVILISH DIFFERENCE

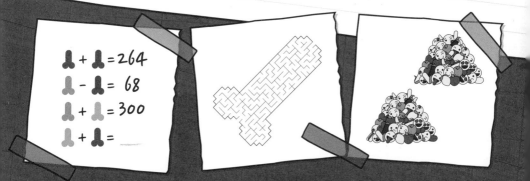

Delve in and discover cock-the-differences,
cock-tastic colouring and all kinds of phallic fun!

## LET'S GET STARTED!

Help Spermy
find his way!

# RUDE SEARCH

Find the 8 hidden words

```
      A N P O C
    I P A W D O P
  M L C A P H F Z P
  J I B O G P E X D
  K P D C C P W P A
  P J O N P K P A P
  G F D E U P O P Q
  Z P B C B V P Y P
  S H A F T K C D P
  Y N L M L B S I R
  T X L A R P A C B
  A W B S C U T K S
  C B A D V H A P D
  D D G E I R F R P
  C E P G E F D P Q
  D P E P F V F P P
  J O H N S O N P T
  Y A L G L F P Q P
  F H G D P E G H O
  P K P J H P I P P
  J L B J P D H I S
 K P U L O U J P O N T O O
T V D K P N P M I Z N P M Q X
V C M E M B E R P M A P G N N O H
B S L P S R R P R P Y P Z Q P X O
T P X U L W B M   A V P N Y W G P
 E D C U Y P         Z V P F Y E
  Z X P E             D P W F
```

1. Cock
2. Shaft
3. Ballbag
4. Dong
5. Member
6. Boner
7. Dick
8. Johnson

Find the 8 hidden words

```
        A W D O P
        C A P H F Z P
    I N O G E P A W S
    D C N M L S A Z X
    K P D C C P W P M
    O O I D D Y T U B
    L M E A E Y H K L
    Z P B C B V P Y W
    X C D Y M C C F Y
    R D G D S E W F F
    M B V C Y E A S D
    B D S W Y M G T T
    F X D M P U U E D
    Q D G E I R F R P
    Q A S U C S T C Q
    D P A C K A G E C
    Y E U D S Y N P T
    Y S S E T D I N G
    F B A U O I R O L
    P A G T E R I P P
    Y D E S S D H I S
  A T T A N N O I W V E G G
 T V D H P T I M I L A Y O G H
N C C R O D O L O D I B N A S O N
Y S U C N V R T N P T U Z G P X O
L T M B E R C Q   S T I F F Y G D
  E E C D C E       Z V P W Q E
  W V V B           D N M Y
```

1. Meat
2. Package
3. Python
4. Rod
5. Sausage
6. Stiffy
7. Wand
8. Wang

# COCK-THE-DIFFERENCE

Spot the 5
differences
and spot
the cock!

1. The word "penis" derives from the Latin word for...

a) Tube   b) Finger   c) Worm   d) Tail

2. On average, how many times will a man ejaculate in his lifetime?

a) 2,100   b) 3,400   c) 7,200   d) 9,800

3. The smallest human penis in recorded history was...

a) 9.9 mm   b) 12.6 mm   c) 15.8 mm   d) 18.2 mm

4. It takes around how much blood for the human penis to become stiff?

a) 90ml   b) 130ml   c) 170ml   d) 210ml

General Knowledge

5. On average, men have around how many erections per day?

a) 8    b) 9    c) 10    d) 11

6. The average semen ejaculation contains around
   how many calories?

   a) 1-7    b) 8-15    c) 16-23    d) 24-31

7. The penis is a muscle.

a) True    b) False

8. Which country celebrates the penis each year with
   a dedicated festival?

a) Holland  b) Norway  c) Tunisia  d) Japan

# RUDE SQUARE

Find 3 nicknames for penis that use the red letter

_____ _____ _____
_____ _____ _____
_____ _____

| A | M | W |
|---|---|---|
| N | O | O |
| G | H | D |

| B | N | D |
|---|---|---|
| E | O | C |
| R | K | C |

_____ _____
_____ _____
_____ _____

Find 3 nicknames for penis that use the red letter

| | | |
|---|---|---|
| T | H | D |
| R | **I** | G |
| P | K | C |

| | | |
|---|---|---|
| B | A | W |
| A | **A** | N |
| D | N | G |

# SPOT THE NOT-COCK

Find 5 pears

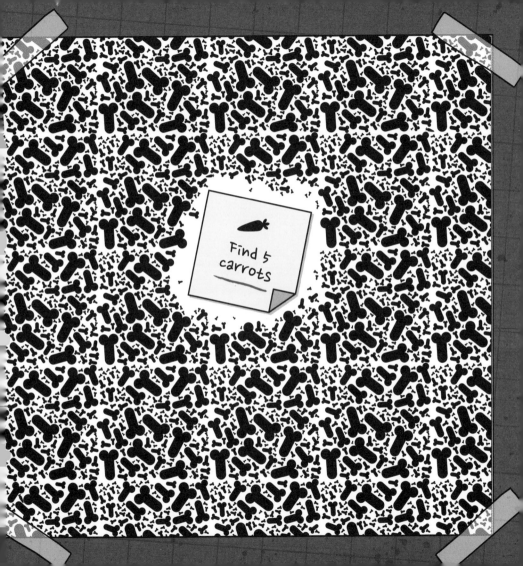

# COCKY CALCULUS

🍆 × 🍆 × 🍆 = 216

🍆 × 🍆 + 🍆 = 20

🍆 × 🍆 + 🍆 = 49

🍆 × 🍆 + 🍆 = _____

🍆 × 🍆 × 🍆 = 125

🍆 × 🍆 + 🍆 = 90

🍆 × 🍆 + 🍆 = 126

🍆 × 🍆 + 🍆 = _____

🍆 + 🍆 × 🍆 = 30

🍆 × 🍆 − 🍆 = 56

🍆 × 🍆 + 🍆 = 24

🍆 + 🍆 × 🍆 = _____

🍆 + 🍆 × 🍆 = 98

🍆 × 🍆 − 🍆 = 12

🍆 × 🍆 + 🍆 = 96

🍆 + 🍆 × 🍆 = _____

$$\blacksquare \times \blacksquare \times \blacksquare = 343$$
$$\blacksquare \times \blacksquare + \blacksquare = 12$$
$$\blacksquare \times \blacksquare + \blacksquare = 32$$
$$\blacksquare \times \blacksquare + \blacksquare = \underline{\hphantom{000}}$$

$$\blacksquare \times \blacksquare \times \blacksquare = 64$$
$$\blacksquare \times \blacksquare + \blacksquare = 156$$
$$\blacksquare \times \blacksquare + \blacksquare = 29$$
$$\blacksquare \times \blacksquare + \blacksquare = \underline{\hphantom{000}}$$

$$\blacksquare + \blacksquare \times \blacksquare = 60$$
$$\blacksquare \times \blacksquare - \blacksquare = 42$$
$$\blacksquare \times \blacksquare + \blacksquare = 56$$
$$\blacksquare + \blacksquare \times \blacksquare = \underline{\hphantom{000}}$$

$$\blacksquare + \blacksquare \times \blacksquare = 72$$
$$\blacksquare \times \blacksquare - \blacksquare = 30$$
$$\blacksquare \times \blacksquare + \blacksquare = 42$$
$$\blacksquare + \blacksquare \times \blacksquare = \underline{\hphantom{000}}$$

# COCK-TO-DOT

Join the dots to reveal some funky patterns

35• 33• •38 •36

30• 34• •37 •41

29• 32• 31• 27• •44 •40 •39 •42

25• •46

26• 28• •43 •45

22• 24• •47 •49

23• 21• •50 •48

19• •52

17• •54

14• 20• •51 •57

15• 18• •53 •56

3• 1• 11• •60 •70 •68

16• 12• •59 •55

2• 6• 4• 7• 13• •58 •64 •67 •65 •69

5• 8• •63 •66

10• 9• •62 •61

Join the dots to reveal some funky patterns

94 · 93 · 61 · 60 ·

95 · 92 · 62 · 59 ·

130 · 129 · 96 · 91 · 63 · 58 · 25 ·

128 · 97 · 90 · 64 · 57 · 26 ·

127 · 98 · 89 · 65 · 56 · 27 ·

126 · 99 · 88 · 66 · 55 · 28 ·

125 · 100 · 87 · 67 · 54 · 29 ·

124 · 101 · 86 · 68 · 53 · 30 ·

123 · 102 · 85 · 69 · 52 · 31 ·

122 · 103 · 84 · 70 · 51 · 32 ·

121 · 104 · 83 · 71 · 50 · 33 ·

120 · 105 · 82 · 72 · 49 · 34 · 24 ·

145 · 144 · 131 · 119 · 106 · 81 · 73 · 48 · 35 · 23 · 10 ·

146 · 143 · 132 · 118 · 107 · 80 · 74 · 47 · 36 · 22 · 11 · 9 ·

153 · 147 · 142 · 133 · 117 · 108 · 79 · 75 · 46 · 37 · 21 · 12 · 8 · 1 ·

152 · 148 · 141 · 134 · 116 · 109 · 78 · 76 · 45 · 38 · 20 · 13 · 7 · 2 ·

151 · 149 · 140 · 135 · 115 · 110 · 77 · 44 · 39 · 19 · 14 · 6 · 3 ·

150 · 139 · 136 · 114 · 111 · 43 · 40 · 18 · 15 · 5 · 4 ·

138 · 137 · 113 · 112 · 42 · 41 · 17 · 16 ·

# INSULT GENERATOR

Simply choose a number from each column to generate your insult

1. Massive
2. Wonky
3. Lanky
4. Floppy
5. Slippery
6. Shrivelled
7. Huge
8. Sloppy
9. Bumpy
10. Wrinkly

1. Wet
2. Hairy
3. Filthy
4. Smelly
5. Flaky
6. Wobbly
7. Moist
8. Veiny
9. Sweaty
10. Sticky

1. Fanny
2. Cock
3. Flange
4. Meat
5. Nipple
6. Butt
7. Willy
8. Helmet
9. Boob
10. Ball

1. Head
2. Licker
3. Face
4. Juggler
5. Hole
6. Smeller
7. Rubber
8. Blaster
9. Hugger
10. Tickler

Help Spermy find his **hat** for his big date

# RUDE SEARCH

Find the 8 hidden words

```
      F D S A O
    I K F W D A S
  M H O N S R F Z S
  J I B A O S E W D
  L S R O K B W E F
  S J A D S L B I S
  G F D E U U A N W
  Z S J O J V S E S
  U R F F T L K R S
  Y D H M K A T U R
  T Z H F N S F S J
  F W W S O U T O S
  O J F O V H F S D
  D D G I O R F R S
  O M S G I D D S W
  D S A S F V S R S
  J A H N S A C S T
  Y F K G H F H W S
  F H G D S O L H A
  W L S B H W O S S
  J H B J S D N D S
L P R I C K J S G R T A A
T V D L S D N M I Z D S M W Z
V O M E K W I L L Y F S G R D A H
J S H S U R R B R S Y S Z W S Z A
T S Z U H W J M   F V W D Y W G S
 I D O U Y S      Z V S F Y D
 Z Z S X          D S W F
```

1. Wood
2. Manhood
3. Snake
4. Schlong
5. Willy
6. Weiner
7. Knob
8. Prick

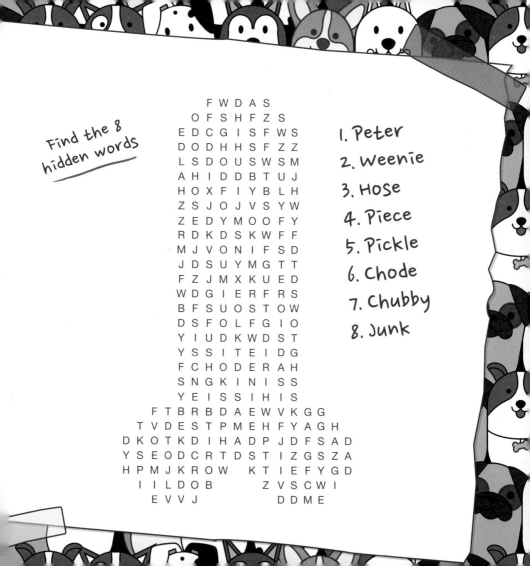

Find the 8 hidden words

```
        F W D A S
      O F S H F Z S
    E D C G I S F W S
    D O D H H S F Z Z
    L S D O U S W S M
    A H I D D B T U J
    H O X F I Y B L H
    Z S J O J V S Y W
    Z E D Y M O O F Y
    R D K D S K W F F
    M J V O N I F S D
    J D S U Y M G T T
    F Z J M X K U E D
    W D G I E R F R S
    B F S U O S T O W
    D S F O L F G I O
    Y I U D K W D S T
    Y S S I T E I D G
    F C H O D E R A H
    S N G K I N I S S
    Y E I S S I H I S
  F T B R B D A E W V K G G
  T V D E S T P M E H F Y A G H
D K O T K D I H A D P J D F S A D
Y S E O D C R T D S T I Z G S Z A
H P M J K R O W   K T I E F Y G D
  I I L D O B       Z V S C W I
    E V V J           D D M E
```

1. Peter
2. Weenie
3. Hose
4. Piece
5. Pickle
6. Chode
7. Chubby
8. Junk

Spot the 5 differences

and spot the cock!

# ANAGRAMS

Unscramble these rude riddles!

## DEERNUTS

Hint: Place them in your mouth

_____

## SHITPOLL

Hint: Keep going up

_____

## NOBALARM

Hint: Doesn't look right

_____

# SUCKTIME

Hint: So filthy

___ ___ ___ ___ ___ ___ ___ ___

# BUMDATER

Hint: Give it a few taps

___ ___ ___ ___ ___ ___ ___ ___

# GIANTNIPS

Hint: Keep them on the wall

___ ___ ___ ___ ___ ___ ___ ___ ___

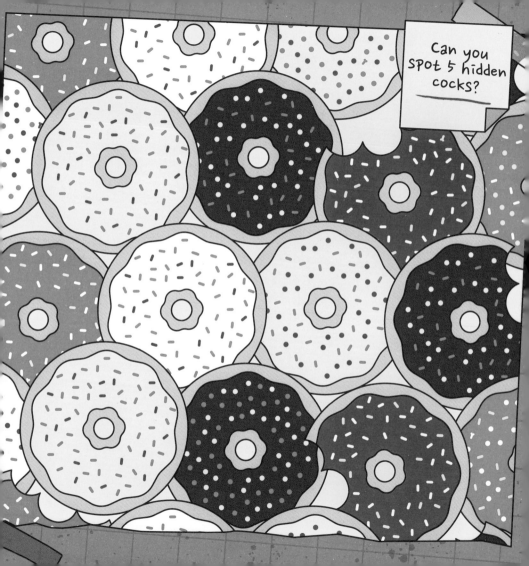

Science and nature

Bird              Aploparaksis Turdi

Fish              Colon Rectum

Octopus          Dik-dik

Beetle           Slippery Dick

Tapeworm       Tufted Titmouse

Antelope        Wunderpus Photogenicus

Match up
the animals
with their
rude names

Cactus                          Stiffcock

Mushroom                        Shagbark

Flower                          Family Jewels

Milkweed                        Shaggy Soldier

Shrub                           Boob

Tree                            Phallus Impudicus

Match up
the plants
with their
rude names

# COCKY CALCULUS

Solve these mind-boggling equations

$360 \div $ 🔵 $= 45$

$83 \times $ 🔵 $= 332$

$445 - $ 🔵 $= 128$

$237 + $ 🔵 $= 328$

$546 \div $ ⍦ $= 45$

$8 \times $ ⍦ $= 104$

$211 - $ ⍦ $= 35$

$417 + $ ⍦ $= 516$

🔵 $= \underline{\quad}$   🔵 $= \underline{\quad}$   🔵 $= \underline{\quad}$   🔵 $= \underline{\quad}$

⍦ $= \underline{\quad}$   ⍦ $= \underline{\quad}$   ⍦ $= \underline{\quad}$   ⍦ $= \underline{\quad}$

Solve these
mind-boggling equations

161 ÷ ♦ = 7          121 × ♦ = 605

323 − ♦ = 82         141 + ♦ = 282

64 ÷ ♈ = 16          45 × ♈ = 135

378 − ♈ = 253        78 + ♈ = 238


♦ = ___    ♦ = ___    ♦ = ___    ♦ = ___

♈ = ___    ♈ = ___    ♈ = ___    ♈ = ___

Join the dots
to reveal some
funky patterns

• 45    • 48    • 49

• 41    • 44

• 37    • 40                    • 50

• 36                            • 47

• 33                            • 46

• 32                            • 43

• 29                            • 42

• 28                            • 39

• 25                            • 38

• 24                            • 35

• 21                            • 34

• 20

• 13    • 16    • 17

• 9    • 12

• 5    • 8

• 4                                                                      • 31

• 1                    • 14    • 15                        • 27    • 30

                       • 11                          • 23    • 26

• 2    • 3    • 6    • 7    • 10              • 18    • 19    • 22

Join the dots to reveal some funky patterns

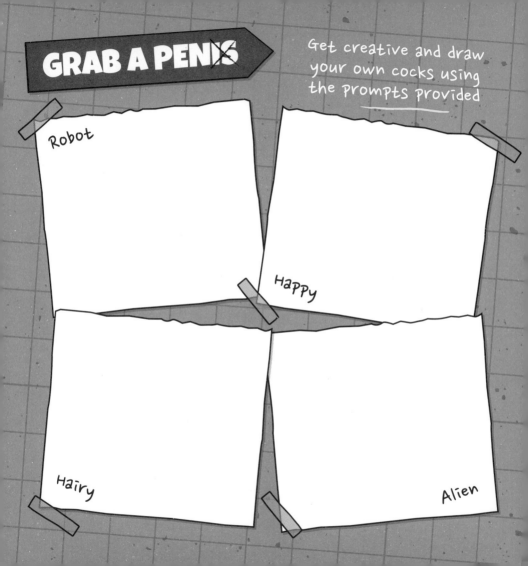

# GET COLOURING

Grab some crayons and spot the cock!

Grab some crayons and spot the cock!

Match up 3 sets of identical pairs

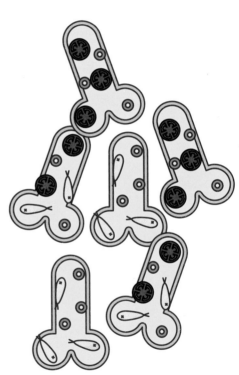

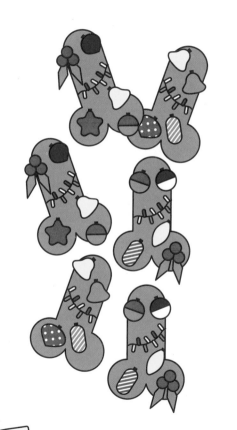

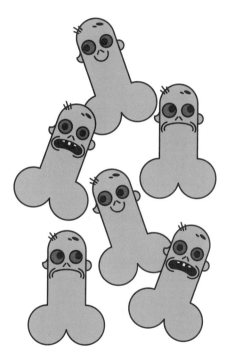

# COCK-THE-DIFFERENCE

Spot the 5 differences

and spot the cock!

Spot the 5 differences

and spot the cock!

Finish the 5 vagina nicknames using the <u>missing letters</u>

| M | I | N | G | E |   |
|---|---|---|---|---|---|
| M |   |   | F |   |   |
|   | A |   |   | Y |   |
| T |   | C |   |   |   |
|   |   | A |   | R |   |

O E U N
N F V F
A B E

Finish the 5 cocky nicknames using the missing letters

Missing letters provided: I E E M E / B H P E K / L K W

Completed answers:

- P **E** C **K** E R → **PECKER**
- **K** N O **B** → **KNOB**
- **W** **I** L **L** Y → **WILLY**
- C **H** O **P** P **E** R → **CHOPPER**
- **M** **E** M B **E** R → **MEMBER**

Find 5
mushrooms

# COCKY CALCULUS

Solve these
mind-boggling equations

🍆 + 🍆 = 264

🍆 − 🍆 = 68

🍆 + 🍆 = 300

🍆 + 🍆 = _____

🍆 + 🍆 = 312

🍆 − 🍆 = 60

🍆 + 🍆 = 260

🍆 + 🍆 = _____

🦴 × 🦴 = 169

🦴 + 🦴 = 108

🦴 + 🦴 = 58

🦴 + 🦴 = _____

🦴 × 🦴 = 144

🦴 + 🦴 = 240

🦴 + 🦴 = 36

🦴 + 🦴 = _____

🔵 + 🔵 = 508      🔵 + 🔵 = 312

🟢 − 🔵 = 70      🔵 − 🔵 = 37

🟢 + 🟡 = 404     🔵 + 🟡 = 316

🟡 + 🔵 = ___     🟡 + 🔵 = ___


🔵 × 🔵 = 64      🔵 × 🔵 = 121

🟡 + 🟡 = 176     🟡 + 🟡 = 202

🟡 + 🔵 = 26      🟡 + 🔵 = 182

🟡 + 🟡 = ___     🟡 + 🟡 = ___

Grab some crayons and spot the cock!

Grab some crayons and spot the cock!

# BLINDFOLD ART

Try to finish these cheeky drawings while blindfolded

Try to finish these cheeky drawings while blindfolded

Help Spermy find his **slippers** for his cosy night in

General knowledge

1. On average, how many erections do men get each night?

a) 4      b) 6        c) 8      d) 10

2. One in how many men are able to give themselves oral sex?

a) 400    b) 800    c) 1,200    d) 1,600

3. Ithyphallophobia is a fear of a what kind of penis?

a) Veiny    b) Animal    c) Hairy    d) Erect

4. "cock shot" and "beaver" are terms used in what game?

a) Checkers    b) Golf    c) Backgammon    d) Squash

5. What organ expands by around 10 times its size on emotional stimulus?

a) Penis   b) Rectum   c) Tongue   d) Pupil

6. How many penises does a male snake have?

a) 0   b) 1   c) 2   d) 3

7. The hole on a violin goes by what name?

a) A-hole   b) F-hole   c) P-hole   d) B-hole

8. "Dump" and "floater" are terms used in what game?

a) Table tennis   b) Hockey   c) Rugby   d) Volleyball

# COCK-THE-DIFFERENCE

Spot the 5 differences

and spot the cock!

# COCKY CALCULUS

Solve these
mind-boggling *equations*

$328 \div$ 🔴 $= 82$         $99 \times$ 🔵 $= 495$

$72 -$ 🔵 $= 11$         $167 +$ 🔴 $= 200$

$252 \div$ 🔵 $= 42$         $19 \times$ 🔵 $= 133$

$892 -$ 🔵 $= 762$         $78 +$ 🔴 $= 167$

🔴 $=$ \_\_\_     🔴 $=$ \_\_\_     🔵 $=$ \_\_\_     🔴 $=$ \_\_\_

🔵 $=$ \_\_\_     🔵 $=$ \_\_\_     🔵 $=$ \_\_\_     🔴 $=$ \_\_\_

Solve these
mind-boggling <u>equations</u>

$121 \div$ 🔵 $= 11$      $222 \times$ 🔵 $= 888$

$398 -$ 🔵 $= 145$      $62 +$ 🔵 $= 176$

$117 \div$ 🔵 $= 9$      $57 \times$ 🔵 $= 228$

$89 -$ 🔵 $= 13$      $562 +$ 🔵 $= 620$

🔵 $=$ _____    🔵 $=$ _____    🔵 $=$ _____    🔵 $=$ _____

🔵 $=$ _____    🔵 $=$ _____    🔵 $=$ _____    🔵 $=$ _____

# ANAGRAMS

Unscramble these
rude riddles!

## SENDBUMS

Hint: Nice and thick

_ _ _ _ _ _ _ _

## FREEDUMP

Hint: Smells lovely

_ _ _ _ _ _ _ _

## GIANTLOG

Hint: Nothing to be proud of

_ _ _ _ _ _ _ _

Unscramble these
rude riddles!

# LIKEWANG

Hint: A bit floppy

_ _ _ _ _ _ _ _

# TASTENIP

Hint: One at a time please

_ _ _ _ _ _ _ _

# NEATPOLE

Hint: Horny

_ _ _ _ _ _ _ _

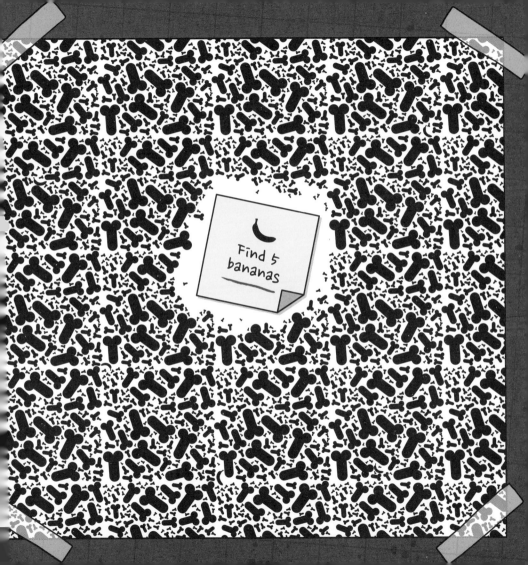

Find 5
bananas

# WHAT SIZE ARE THEY?

Do you know the average size of each animal's <u>member</u>?

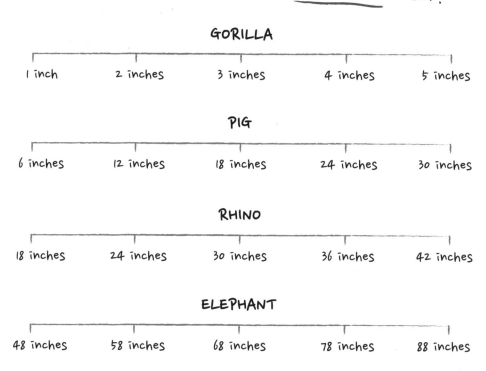

### GORILLA

| 1 inch | 2 inches | 3 inches | 4 inches | 5 inches |

### PIG

| 6 inches | 12 inches | 18 inches | 24 inches | 30 inches |

### RHINO

| 18 inches | 24 inches | 30 inches | 36 inches | 42 inches |

### ELEPHANT

| 48 inches | 58 inches | 68 inches | 78 inches | 88 inches |

Do you know the average size
of each animal's member?

## DUCK

| 3 inches | 6 inches | 9 inches | 12 inches | 15 inches |

## CAT

| 0.2 inches | 0.5 inches | 0.8 inches | 1.1 inches | 1.4 inches |

## BLUE WHALE

| 80 inches | 90 inches | 100 inches | 110 inches | 120 inches |

## HORSE

| 5 inches | 10 inches | 15 inches | 20 inches | 25 inches |

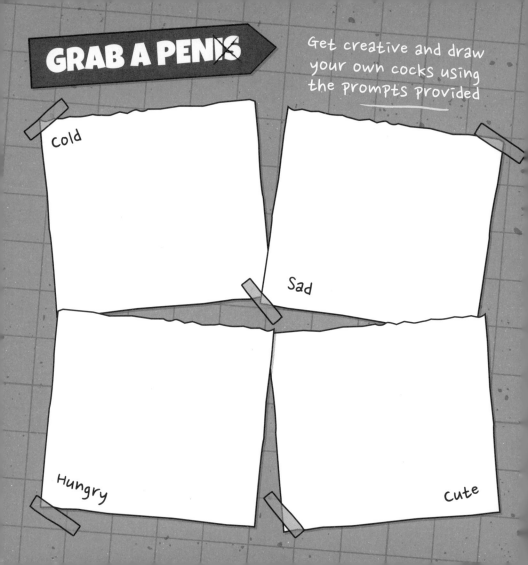

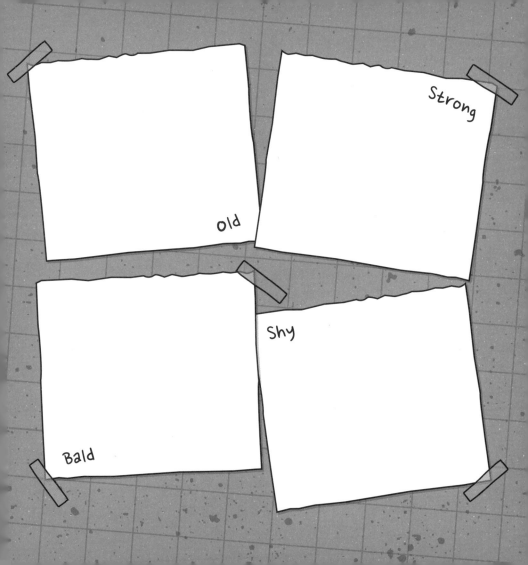

Match up 3 sets of identical pairs

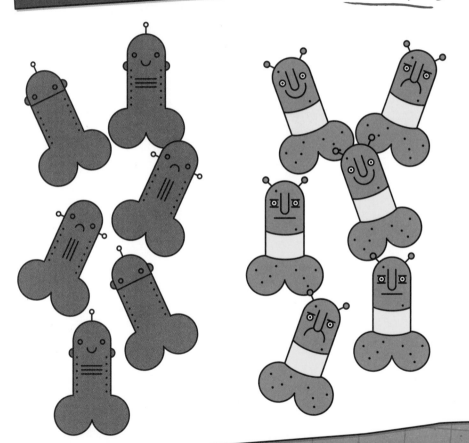

Match up 3 sets
of identical pairs

Finish 5 boob nicknames
using the missing letters

| J |   | G |   |   |
|---|---|---|---|---|
|   | I |   |   |   |
| B |   |   | S |   |
| T |   |   | A | S |
| T |   |   | N | S |

T U I T
S S A W
T P A

Finish 5 cocky nicknames using the missing letters

Grid:

| | O | H | | | O | |
|---|---|---|---|---|---|---|
| | O | | E | R | | |
| R | O | | | | | |
| | U | | K | | | |
| D | | N | | | | |

J N D O
S B J N
G N N

## HELP SPERMY!

# ANSWERS

## SPOT THE COCKS

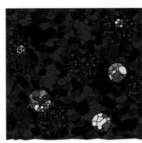
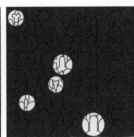

## RUDE SEARCH

```
        A N P O C              A W D O P
    I P A W D O P            C A P H F Z P
  M L C A P H F Z P        I N O G E P A W S
  J I B O G P E X D        D C N M L S A Z X
  K P D C C P W P A        K P D C C P W P M
  P J O N P K P A P        O O I D D Y T U B
  G F D E U P O P Q        L M E A E Y H K L
  Z P B C B V P Y P        Z P B C B V P Y W
  S H A F T K C D P        X C D Y M C C F Y
  Y N L M L B S I R        R D G D S E W F F
  T X L A R P A C B        M B V C Y E A S D
  A W B S C U T K S        B D S W Y M G T T
  C B A D V H A P D        F X D M P U U E D
  D O G E I R F R P        Q D G E I R F R P
  C E P G E F D P Q        Q A S U C S T C Q
  D P E P F V F P P        D P A C K A G E C
  J O H N S O N P T        Y E U D S Y N P T
  Y A L G L F P Q P        Y S B E T D I N G
  F H G D P E G H O        F B A U O I R O L
  P K P J H P I P P        P A G T E R I P P
  J L B J P D H I S        Y D E S S D H I S
  K P U L O U J P O N T O O      A T T A N N O I W V E G G
  T V D K P N P M I Z N P M Q X  T V D H P T I M I L A Y O G H
  V C M E M B E R P M A P Q N N O H  N C C R O D O L D I T B N A S O N
  B S L P S R R P R P Y P Z Q P X O  Y S U C N V R T N P T U Z G P X O
  T P X U L W B M   A V P N Y W G P  L T M B E R C Q   S T I F F Y G D
  E D C U Y P       Z V P F Y E      E E C D C E       Z V P W Q E
  Z X P E           D P W F          W V V B           D N M Y
```

## COCK-THE-DIFFERENCE

## PUB QUIZ | GENERAL KNOWLEDGE

Question 1. = d) Tail

Question 2. = c) 7,200

Question 3. = a) 9.9 mm

Question 4. = b) 130ml

Question 5. = d) 11

Question 6. = a) 1-7

Question 7. = b) False

Question 8. = d) Japan

## RUDE SQUARE

| | | |
|---|---|---|
| A | M | W |
| N | O | O |
| G | H | D |

DONG
MANHOOD
WOOD

| | | |
|---|---|---|
| T | H | D |
| R | I | G |
| P | K | C |

DICK
GIRTH
PRICK

| | | |
|---|---|---|
| B | N | D |
| E | O | C |
| R | K | C |

BONER
COCK
ROD

| | | |
|---|---|---|
| B | A | W |
| A | A | N |
| D | N | G |

BANANA
WAND
WANG

## SPOT THE NOT-COCK

## COCKY CALCULUS

$$\text{🍆} \times \text{🍆} + \text{🍆} = 31$$
$$\text{🍆} \times \text{🍆} + \text{🍆} = 56$$
$$\text{🍆} + \text{🍆} \times \text{🍆} = 28$$
$$\text{🍆} + \text{🍆} \times \text{🍆} = 55$$
$$\text{🍆} \times \text{🍆} + \text{🍆} = 25$$
$$\text{🍆} \times \text{🍆} + \text{🍆} = 53$$
$$\text{🍆} + \text{🍆} \times \text{🍆} = 50$$
$$\text{🍆} + \text{🍆} \times \text{🍆} = 42$$

## COCK-TO-DOT

## HELP SPERMY!

ANSWERS

# ANSWERS

## RUDE SEARCH

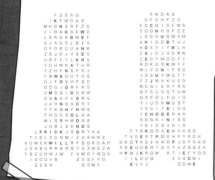

## SPOT THE COCKS

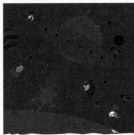

## COCK-THE-DIFFERENCE

## ANAGRAMS

DEERNUTS = DENTURES

SHITPOLL = HILLTOPS

NOBALARM = ABNORMAL

SUCKTIME = MUCKIEST

BUMDATER = DRUMBEAT

GIANTNIPS = PAINTINGS

## SPOT THE COCKS

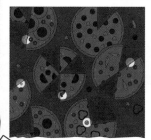 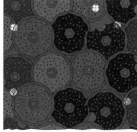

## PUB QUIZ | SCIENCE AND NATURE

### ANIMALS

Bird = Tufted Titmouse
Fish = Slippery Dick
Octopus = Wunderpus Photogenicus
Beetle = Colon Rectum
Tapeworm = Aploparaksis Turdi
Antelope = Dik-dik

### PLANTS

Cactus = Boob
Mushroom = Phallus Impudicus
Flower = Shaggy Soldier
Milkweed = Family Jewels
Shrub = Stiffcock
Tree = Shagbark

## COCKY CALCULUS

🍆 = 8   🍆 = 4   🍆 = 317   🍆 = 91
🍆 = 6   🍆 = 13  🍆 = 176   🍆 = 99

🍆 = 7   🍆 = 5   🍆 = 241   🍆 = 141
🍆 = 4   🍆 = 3   🍆 = 125   🍆 = 160

## COCK-TO-DOT

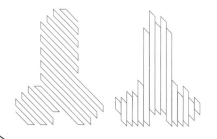

## ANSWERS

# ANSWERS

## WHAT A PAIR!

## SPOT THE COCKS

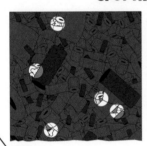 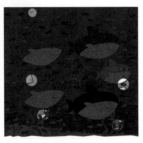

## COCK-THE-DIFFERENCE

## PUB QUIZ | GEOGRAPHY

### UK

- Cocks
- Dick Place
- Fingringhoe
- Lower Swell
- Netherthong
- Shitterton
- Twatt
- Wetwang

### US

- Balltown
- Beaver City
- Comertown
- Dickshooter
- Hooker
- Ramtown
- Sugar Tit
- Three Way

# ANSWERS

## SPOT THE NOT-COCK

## FINISH IT OFF

| M | I | N | G | E |
| M | U | F | F |   |
| F | A | N | N | Y |
| T | A | C | O |   |
| B | E | A | V | E | R |

| P | E | C | K | E | R |
| K | N | O | B |   |
| W | I | L | L | Y |
| C | H | O | P | P | E | R |
| M | E | M | B | E | R |

## HELP SPERMY!

## COCKY CALCULUS

$$\text{🍆} + \text{🍆} = 232$$
$$\text{👕} + \text{👕} = 99$$

$$\text{🍆} + \text{🍆} = 334$$
$$\text{👕} + \text{👕} = 106$$

$$\text{🍆} + \text{🍆} = 200$$
$$\text{🍆} + \text{👕} = 144$$

$$\text{🍆} + \text{🍆} = 279$$
$$\text{👕} + \text{👕} = 272$$

## COCK-THE-DIFFERENCE

## COCKY CALCULUS

$\phi$ = 4   $\phi$ = 5   $\phi$ = 61   $\phi$ = 33

$\Upsilon$ = 6   $\Upsilon$ = 7   $\Upsilon$ = 130   $\Upsilon$ = 89

$\phi$ = 11   $\phi$ = 4   $\phi$ = 253   $\phi$ = 114

$\Upsilon$ = 13   $\Upsilon$ = 4   $\Upsilon$ = 76   $\Upsilon$ = 58

## SPOT THE NOT-COCK

## ANAGRAMS

SENDBUMS = DUMBNESS

FREEDUMP = PERFUMED

GIANTLOG = GLOATING

LIKEWANG = WEAKLING

TASTENIP = PATIENTS

NEATPOLE = ANTELOPE

# ANSWERS

# ANSWERS

## WHAT A PAIR!

## WHAT SIZE ARE THEY?

GORILLA = 2 inches

PIG = 12 inches

RHINO = 24 inches

ELEPHANT = 78 inches

DUCK = 9 inches

CAT = 0.2 inches

BLUE WHALE = 120 inches

HORSE = 20 inches

## FINISH IT OFF

| J | U | G | S |   |   |   |
|---|---|---|---|---|---|---|
| T | I | T | S |   |   |   |
| B | A | P | S |   |   |   |
| T | A | T | A | S |   |   |
| T | W | I | N | S |   |   |

| J | O | H | N | S | O | N |
|---|---|---|---|---|---|---|
| B | O | N | E | R |   |   |
| R | O | D |   |   |   |   |
| J | U | N | K |   |   |   |
| D | O | N | G |   |   |   |

Always check for lumps.
Sincerely yours,
Balls & Boobs

## Spot the Cock
Jason Murphy

Hardback

978-1-78783-590-0

They seek them here, they seek them there, these cocks are simply everywhere! But are you beady-eyed enough to find these one-eyed trouser snakes in different locations? From the deepest depths of space to shark-infested waters, hone your sleuthing skills in this wickedly funny and ever-so-slightly naughty search-and-find book.

DEDICATED TO CHRIS, KELLY
& MY LONG-SUFFERING WIFE, SAM.

Have you enjoyed this book?

If so, find us on Facebook at
**Summersdale Publishers**, on Twitter at
**@Summersdale** and on Instagram and TikTok at
**@summersdalebooks** and get in touch.

We'd love to hear from you!

**www.summersdale.com**